✦ The 69th Infantry Regiment from Trier parading before the war.

1914

✦ THE MARNE – THE GERMAN ARMY STOPPED AT THE GATES OF PARIS ... p. 2
The Prussian infantryman in August 1914 ... p. 3
Kit inspection ... p. 4
Personal equipment ... p. 5
The Pickelhaube, a much sought after war souvenir ... p. 6

1915

Belt buckles ... p. 8
The war lingers on ... p. 9
The infantryman of Notre-Dame-de-Lorette ... p. 10
Shortages and ersatz ... p. 11
Individual weapons : rifles ... p. 12
Handguns ... p. 13

1916

✦ A MACHINE-GUNNER AT LESEPARGES ... p. 14
Verdun : the breakthrough fails ... p. 15
The Stahlhelm 16 replaces the Pickelhaube ... p. 16
Individual weapons : grenades ... ... p. 18
... and combat knives ... p. 19
MG 08/15 crew man : Mort-Homme hill, Verdun ... p. 20

1917

✦ STILL ALL QUIET ON THE WESTERN FRONT ... p. 21
Collective weapons ... p. 22
MG accessories ... p. 23
Collective weapons : the MG 08/15 ... p. 24
NCO machine-gun crew commander ... p. 25

1918

✦ GERMANS AT THE GATES OF PARIS ONCE MORE ... p. 26
The Sturmtruppen ... p. 27
The infantryman of the Ludendorff offensive ... p. 28
A new weapon : tanks ... p. 29
Trench artillery ... p. 30
Medals and awards ... p. 31
Conclusion ... p. 32
Acknowledgements ... p. 33

THE MARNE – THE GERMAN ARMY STOPPED AT THE GATES OF PARIS

In 1914, with its 69 million-strong population, Germany was a powerful nation in which the imperial army played an important role.

Indeed, after the victory of 1870 that helped, among other things, unify the country, it was largely agreed to make the army more modern and efficient. Contrary to its European neighbours, Germany did not have a colonial empire as big as that of the French or British.

The war against France in 1870 had led to the annexation of the Alsace and of a part of the Lorraine, but economically, Germany depended on imports when it came to the raw materials necessary for its powerful industry.

The alliance with Austria-Hungary and Italy in 1882 helped the country defend its borders. France reacted quickly by signing an alliance with Russia in 1894 ; Great Britain followed suit in 1904.

As a consequence, all the protagonists were in place by 1907 : the Triple Entente (France, Great Britain and Russia) on one side, and the Triple Alliance (Germany, Austria-Hungary and Italy) on the other.

The entire mechanism was set in motion on 28 June 1914 when Franz Ferdinand, Austria-Hungary's heir, was assassinated in Sarajevo.

Germany declared war on Russia on 1 August and France on the 3rd.

The German plan of action, conceived by General Von Schlieffen, the chief of staff, started with the invasion of Belgium, in order to bypass the French Army from the north and then to attack from the flank, thus avoiding France's fortified lines.

Rapidity was key in order to rout the French and British armies, which would allow Germany to subsequently concentrate its troops to counter Russia and to avoid fighting on two different fronts separated by thousands of miles.

Despite a good start, with its numerous victories and the French army's heavy losses, the German army's advance stalled during the first Battle of the Marne.

They were indeed stopped by the French troops, some of whom had travelled by taxi, on September 6th ; the capital was saved.

This setback marked the end of the war of movement and opened a new phase, that of a war of positions, which the Germans so understandably dreaded, since they now had to fight on two fronts.
At the end of 1914, the front line had set, going from the North Sea to the Swiss border.

✦ The capture of Fort Manonviller on August 28th, bombarded for several days by 420mm shells, came as a surprise for the French high staff as the French army did not possess such heavy artillery.

THE PRUSSIAN INFANTRYMAN IN AUGUST 1914

✦ Marching and combat kit consisted of a canvas 1895 haversack (Tornister 95) to which the 1910 mess tin (Kochgeschirr 10) was attached. The 1892 tent section was rolled around the coat. On the lower back, the 1887 bread bag (Brotbeutel 87) was attached to the belt. The 1910 water bottle (Feldflasche 10) was attached to the bag.
In the picture, the bag protruding from the haversack's flap contained the tent pegs and poles.

✦ The 1890 ammunition pouches were still in use at the beginning of the war, especially in reserve units (Landwehr).

✦ The 1890 ammunition pouch is very much visible in this unit preparing to go to war.

1914

✦ This infantryman's equipment is typical of the beginning of the war : an 1895 Pickelhaube, here with its cover, a Feldrock 07/10 tunic, 1910 trousers, 1895 belt with brass buckle, 1909 ammunition pouches.

KIT INSPECTION

At the beginning of the war, the imperial army mobilised 3.8 million men. There were 217 active regiments and 113 reserve regiments that were also to be thrown into the fray.

Infantrymen were equipped with the new 1910 uniform. Being green, it offered far better camouflage than the French uniform. The 1895 Pickelhaube, with its brass fittings, had a plate on the front representing the arms of each state.
This was just an aesthetic element as being made of leather it did not provide any protection against artillery.

The Mauser 1898 (Gewehr 98, 7.92mm) remained the main weapon. It was an excellent rifle which was used throughout the conflict without undergoing any major modifications.

The rounds were carried in 1909 ammunition pouches (Patronentaschen 09), which contained four clips of five bullets each, that is to say sixty rounds per pouch.

The 1887 bread bag (Brotbeutel 87) was used to carry small campaign equipment.

The 1898/05 (Seitengewehr 98/05) bayonet was carried thanks to the 1898 frog.
For eating, the soldiers were equipped with a 1910 mess tin (Kochgeschirr 10) as well as a 1893 water bottle (Feldflasche 93) made of enamelled iron or an aluminium 1907 model.
They carried an 1895 haversack (Tornister 95) with an exterior cow skin cover.
The small 1874 shovel (Spaten 74) was carried in its 1887 carrier.
Contrary to the French, who wore lace-up boots, the Germans had leather 1866 boots (Marschstiefel 66).

Author's note : I have used the English terms to designate each piece of equipment ; the German name is mentioned in brackets. The Germans only used the last two numbers of the year the item was put in service, they never used the term «pattern or model».

✦ The 1893 haversack originally had a «flap» with a cow skin cover. It was removed during the war, and replaced by canvas.

✦ Enamelled iron mess tin with its folding cutlery.

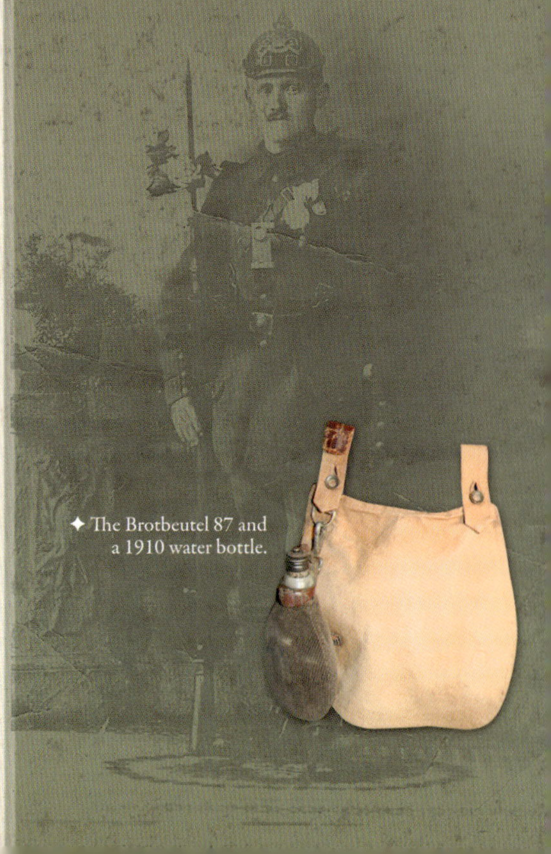

✦ The Brotbeutel 87 and a 1910 water bottle.

PERSONAL EQUIPMENT

Just like the French infantryman, the Landser carried all the equipment necessary for to live on the front line. Aside from regulation equipment, the infantrymen also brought along privately purchased items in order to make life a bit easier.

Family, of course, was of great help, thanks to the Feldpost's (army postal service) efficiency which allowed relatives to send supplies and useful items to the front line throughout the conflict. Letters, the only remaining bond with loved ones, was also very important for morale, despite the fact that Germany did not suffer any material damage during the war, contrary to France.

✦ The 1915 identity tag (Erkennungsmarke 15) was worn on the neck and could be placed in a leather pouch. Top : regulation shoulder straps. Left : a card announcing the death of a soldier.

✦ A military-themed pack of cards for passing time.

✦ This interesting relic found in a trench a few years ago is in fact a moustache comb. Moustaches were in fashion at the time, as seen in the photo below. It goes without saying that all types of facial hair were subsequently banned, since the reliability of gasmasks depended on absolute airtightness.

✦ The Militarpass, the equivalent of the British Army pay book, contained all the soldier's information, including his previous campaigns. This one here belonged to Josef Ternes, who fought on the Somme and received the Iron Cross (2nd class) in 1917. The booklet on the right was a Franco-German conversation guide that also belonged to Ternes.

✦ Tobacco provided a much-appreciated form of comfort at the time. Note the case with the Kaiser's gift of cigar for the end of 1914-1915.

THE PICKELHAUBE, A MUCH

✦ A Pickelhaube 95 with its brass fittings. The helmet here is adorned with the Prussian front plate as well as the black and white Prussian cockade.

✦ Same helmet, but the 1915 wartime-made pattern with its steel fittings. The spike had been removable since June 28th.

✦ Bavaria 1895.

✦ Hesse 1915.

✦ 1915 Guards helmet.

✦ 1895 Guards officer helmet.

SOUGHT AFTER WAR SOUVENIR

✦ Pickelhaube with its 1892 beige-coloured cotton cover.

✦ Another Prussian model, made of felt for economical reasons.

✦ Saxony 1895.

✦ Baden 1895.

✦ 1895 Prussian reserve officer.

✦ Württemberg 1915.

BELT BUCKLES

Just like the Pickelhaube, the 1895 pattern belt (Koppelschloss 95) came with a brass buckle adorned with the state's insignia. This one, made of white metal, bears its state's motto. The Prussian plaque is the most famous one, with the "Gott mit uns" ("God with us") markings. Due to shortages, the brass was quickly replaced with steel.

✦ The belt buckle, just as symbolic as the Pickelhaube, inspired the French Poilus to transform them into various objects, such as tobacco tins, lighters and religious symbols.

✦ Tobacco holder.

✦ 1915 iron buckle.

✦ 1915 iron buckle painted green.

✦ Bavaria 1895, brass.

✦ Navy and colonial troops, 1895.

✦ Prussia 1895, copper.

✦ Bavaria 1915, steel.

✦ Hesse 1895.

✦ Württemberg 1915.

✦ Prussia 1895, brass, with its central nickel silver badge.

✦ Same buckle, but a special edition non-regulation pattern purchased in regimental canteens, mostly made of copper.

✦ White metal buckle exclusive to the LGR 115 (Leib Garde Regiment), Hesse.

✦ Bavaria 1847.

✦ Saxony 1895.

✦ The older, larger pattern of 1847.

✦ Prussian officer, 1895.

✦ Prussian telegrapher, 1915 ; the buckle is wider in order to use it as a support for a telephone wire unwinding device.

THE WAR LINGERS ON

The situation at the end of 1914 was a static, entrenched frontline in which the troops would live from now on.

But the worst thing for Germany was the allied blockade ; indeed the French and British navies were blocking any maritime traffic and preventing Germany from importing goods.
Yet Germany depended on imports for raw materials such as food, due to its weak and reduced colonial empire.

The consequences of this situation were felt on the front lines. Just like France's armies, the imperial army had to use substitutes - the famous Ersatz - to equip and feed its troops.
This period saw leather equipment being replaced with canvas and even nettles to make fabric ...

The 07/10 tunics were gradually replaced with the new, simplified 1915 Bluse. Despite this, the 07/10 tunics were still used throughout the conflict. Even the highly symbolic Pickelhaube suffered from the shortages : leather was replaced with metal, sometimes felt.

War stocks were depleted, and despite being better equipped and armed than the French army, the Germans had to use all available means.

Allied weapons were reused when possible, especially in rear echelon areas.

Concerning military operations, 1915 was the year of large-scale offensives which, despite causing terrible casualty lists, failed to lead to any great advance.

The soldiers learned about their adversaries, observed each other, and despite 1914 ending with truces and fraternisation, these were not widespread.

The dreadful fighting of the Hartmannswillerkopf in the Alsatian Vosges, as well as the fighting in Bois-le-prêtre and Notre-Dame-de-Lorette, remain in the collective consciousness as violence on an unprecedented scale.
The infantry, «the queen of the battlefield", as it was often called, was under constant artillery fire, which forced European tactics to change.

The most dramatic event of 1915 was the use of gas in Ypres on April 22nd to break through the lines. This weapon would become the symbol of the Great War.
From now on, soldiers would have to take this new weapon into account, and equip themselves accordingly.
Here too, Germany was more advanced than the Allies who had not expected this weapon to be used. Nevertheless, on a strictly military level, gas did not have the expected effects, that is to say the large-scale wiping out of enemy troops. Gas was indeed the cause of 10,000 deaths for the French, and of 9,000 Landser for the Germans.

However, gas proved to be a great tool of psychological warfare; it became one of the war's symbols and terrorised troops throughout the conflict.

✦ "The Kaiser called us and we came." The non-commissioned officer in the foreground is proudly displaying the Iron Cross he was awarded in 1914. All these fresh-faced soldiers are wearing the unmodified Feldrock 07/10 tunic. Patriotism and propaganda had such an effect that many young men joined the army before being called up or mobilised.

In general, these recruits remained motivated by their cause. Their first confrontation with the front line came as a shock to a great number of them as they did not expect such conditions. Many untried recruits were killed in the first days of the war. Those who survived the first few weeks ended up being called the Frontschweine - the German equivalent of the PBI (Poor bloody infantry).

THE INFANTRYMAN OF NOTRE-DAME-DE-LORETTE

1915

With his Feldrock 07/10, this soldier is wearing an ersatz Pickelhaube with the iron fittings that replaced brass, a material that was now used in the manufacture of shells.

He also has the traditional Mauser Gewehr 98 rifle, with its bayonet. On the belt, he has the 15 pattern canvas bag containing the tin gas mask case (Gummimaske 15) that was issued to front line troops following April 22nd.

✦ The number on the lid indicates the size of the gas mask.

✦ Canvas gas mask pouch.

✦ Gummimaske 15 with its carrying tin.

✦ The 113rd (Baden) infantry regiment fought in the Notre-Dame-de-Lorette sector. One soldier here has his picture taken with his comrades in the ruins of a building, certainly behind the lines. Their expressions are serious and their rifles never far from them, since they are aware that respite will be short. In an hour or two, they will have to return to the trenches from which they will perhaps never return. Some of these men are smoking their last cigarette.

SHORTAGES AND ERSATZ

The allied blockade stopped all the imports that Germany depended on. In terms of raw materials, shortages of rubber, iron ore and nitrates (necessary for the making of explosives) hit the country hard.

Rationing was consequently established and old metals were recycled, which led to the troops being ordered to requisition and dismantle the bells of the churches in occupied territory.

Here are a few examples of simplified equipment.

✦ Two different Pickelhauben : one made of felt with a leather peak, and the other entirely made of metal, made by Bing. Both eagles are made of steel. It is worth noting that the metal version was equally inefficient as the felt version when it came to protecting the soldier's head.

✦ The ammunition pouches underwent the same treatment. These ones are made of felt.

✦ Water bottle with a nettle-fabric cover.

✦ A large pattern entrenching tool with its pre-war leather cover and its nettle-fabric cover.

✦ Soldiers tried their best to retain something of their humanity. Music helped make the situation more bearable. One soldier is playing a makeshift double bass.

PERSONAL WEAPONS : RIFLES

The basic weapon of the infantry was the Gewehr 98 rifle which was adopted in 1898 and developed by the engineer Paul Mauser. The rifle had a caliber of 7.92mm, [using five-round chargers]; it was well-designed and went through the entire war without undergoing major modifications or being replaced - it was a lot less prone to problems caused by mud and dirt than the French Lebel... Nevertheless, the previous model, Mauser's Gewehr 88, remained in use, especially in machine-gun units.

Only a small number of units such as cavalry and artillery used the shortened version of the Gewehr, the Karabiner 98 (Kar 98), which, thanks to its smaller size, was eventually used by the assault troops, the Stosstruppen. Behind the lines, all weapons were salvaged from arsenals, such as old French Chassepot rifles from the Franco-Prussian war of 1870 and subsequently used by P.O.W. camp guards.

✦ A Gew 98 that bears the marks of war. Shrapnel has obviously taken a chunk out of the wood; the barrel has also been severely damaged.

✦ Bullets embedded in a tree.

✦ The 98/05 bayonet (Seitengewehr 98/05) which was designed to be fixed to the end of the Gew 98. Length : 50 centimetres.

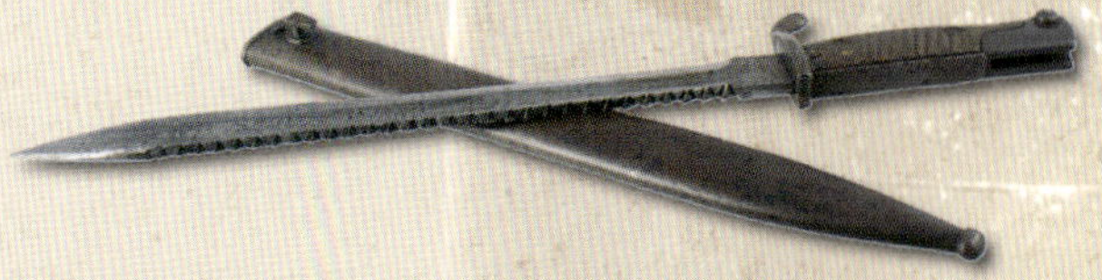

✦ A serrated-edge version of the 98/05 bayonet. Despite rumours spread by French propaganda, this was not a weapon but rather a saw for pioneer units. It is said that German soldiers captured in possession of this bayonet were severely mistreated, sometimes executed, due to the fear it aroused. This bayonet was quickly withdrawn from the front lines.

✦ a. Gewehr 98 - length : 125 cm ; weight : 4.15 kg. It is worth noting that this particular rifle, which was brought home by a French soldier, has been mended with "patches" on its butt.
a. Gewehr 88 - length : 124 cm ; weight : 4 kg.

HANDGUNS

Concerning handguns, the most famous and the most sought after by allied soldiers was the Luger 08 (P08) pistol.
With its 9mm calibre and eight-round magazine, this weapon would gain its reputation in the trenches.

Other than the P08, there was also the Mauser C96, as well as many other handguns that were acquired by the soldiers themselves, either privately purchased or taken from the enemy.

Trench combat led to close-quarter contact with the enemy. Due to the rifle's cumbersome size, handguns became a necessity as they were a lot easier to handle.

✦ A Pistole 08 (or P08). The first 7.65 cal. Luger came out in 1900. After numerous trials and development, the German army adopted the 9mm Luger pistol in August 1908. Two manufacturers produced the weapon as of 1914 : a private company, the DWM, which produced 743,000 between 1909 and 1918, and a national arsenal, Erfurt, with a total production of 519,000 between 1911 and 1918. It is worth mentioning the long-barreled P08 that was issued to the artillery and the navy It was also possible to attach a wooden butt to its handle, just like the C96. The pistol in the photograph has an interesting history. It was found by a French soldier in the Vosges in 1915 who used it until 1918 when he brought it home as a war souvenir. When he fled his home in 1940, he took the gun with him, which ended up hidden in a henhouse, wrapped in a rag ... The small tool was kept in the holster and was used as a screwdriver for various tasks, such as stripping the gun.

✦ The Mauser C96 automatic pistol originally chambered for 7.63 mm bullets. In order to standardise ammunition, it was decided in 1916 to remodel it to take 9mm bullets. To avoid confusion, the number 9 was inscribed on the butt. It was fed via a ten-round clip. The particularity of this pistol is its butt, which serves as a holster. As seen in the top photo, a butt could be fixed to the handle, which allowed greater shooting accuracy. The cleaning rod and a leather pouch containing a spare spring could be fixed to the leather harness. 130,000 were issued during the 4 years of the war.

✦ A Hebel flare-gun with its box of flares. These flares came in different colours, each colour having a specific meaning. They were meant to communicate with the artillery, since radio communication did not exist then. According to the colours, the high command could locate its troops' advances and the artillery could adjust their fire accordingly.

✦ A non-commissioned officer, recognisable thanks to his collar insignia, of the 171st infantry regiment (1917). He is armed with a P08, and has the essential notebook to write down all his observations as well as various forms of punishment. He is wearing an entirely green Mutze 15 and Fernglas 08 binoculars.

✦ The 7.65mm Pistole 07 - otherwise known as the Dreyse 1907 automatic pistol had a seven-round magazine. It was one of the many pistols supplied to the army in order to replace the P08. This weapon was quite complex mechanically. It was designed by L. Schmeisser, who would become famous for the MP38/40 a few years later.

A MACHINE-GUNNER AT LES EPARGES

1916

✦ Two versions of the Fernglas : the Fernglas 08 and the Fernglas 03, both in 6x30.

✦ The Mutze 10 cap was worn behind the lines. A cockade with the colours of the state is placed on the red band, whereas a cockade in the colours of the Empire is placed above it.

✦ In March 1915, a removable grey canvas strip was added in order to conceal the red band.

✦ This 1915 Guards machine-gunner is recognisable thanks to his Pickelhaube, as well as his Mantel 07 greatcoat with its specific Guards Litzen collar insignia. He is identified as belonging to the Guards Grenadier unit by the A on his left shoulder strap. This was an elite unit, that of the Kaiser.

VERDUN : THE BREAKTHROUGH FAILS

In 1916, Germany had been fighting on two different fronts for two years. Due to the alliances, Germany was fighting in France, but also on the Russian front, shared with its Austria-Hungarian allies.

Even though the front lines were stabilised in France, remaining static despite the deadly offensives of 1915, the situation was very different on the Russian front.

The Czar's army had been defeated, allowing Germany and Austria-Hungary to occupy a vast territory. Their victories were emphatic but failed to lead to peace with Russia, but they did allow Germany to move some of its troops to France. The allied blockade kept suffocating the supplies and economy of the country. Germany was in a complicated situation.

Consequently, in 1916, since Russia presented less of a threat, Germany decided to hit the Western Front hard. They chose to attack Verdun on February 21st.

After unprecedented shelling, the French defences were pulverised and a German breakthrough seemed inevitable. Douaumont was taken, but the French succeeded in stopping their advance. 81,000 soldiers died for a 3 to 4 kilometer gain.

Verdun, just like names such as Mort-Homme, hill 304 and Vaux became synonymous with the hellish fighting the soldiers experienced. The violence of the battle was unheard of. The shell fire made men lose their minds, attacks were wiped-out by the never-ending machine-gun fire and avalanches of mortars and grenades - the soldiers of Verdun left the battle wounded both in body and soul.
Almost a century later, the trauma remains present. One only needs to see the number of people visiting the battlefield, amazed at the sight of the trenches, craters and destroyed villages.

On September 2nd, the attack on Verdun was stopped, and the French went back on the offensive. In late December, the battle was considered over.

Simultaneously with Verdun was the Battle of the Somme, which started on July 1st. This time, it was the British who took the initiative. They used a similar tactic, the heavy bombardment of the German lines.

But, just like at Verdun, allied progress was halted. The losses on the evening of July 1st were dreadful : The well-entrenched German lines had survived the bombardment and were able to defend themselves against the attack. This led to huge losses for the British and hardly any ground gained.

1916 thus saw two of the biggest and deadliest battles of the Great War. More than two million soldiers were either killed, wounded, taken prisoner or posted as missing. German troops were exhausted by the fighting. The shortages kept worsening, making life even harder for the Germans, whether on the front line or not.

✦ A group of telephone operators in the Somme, carrying their equipment. The third soldier (from the left) has wrapped his rifle in cloth to protect it from the mud. He is also carrying a reel of cable. A pouch for other telephone equipment is attached to his belt. It is worth noting that the second soldier (from the left) has a K98 that is shorter than the G98, the breech of which is also wrapped in cloth. The two other soldiers on the right are heavily loaded with equipment and ready to return to their trenches.

1916

THE STAHLHELM 16 REPLACES

Even though the infantry's uniform changed the previous year with the introduction of the 1915 pattern tunic, their appearance changed radically in 1916 with the Stahlhelm replacing the Pickelhaube.

The infantry had been wearing the Pickelhaube since 1914. It did not provide any protection against shrapnel, which led to a great number of often fatal head wounds. A few modifications were tried out, in vain, in 1915, when the «Army Detachment Gaede» adopted a steel skull cap. This is why two surgeons, Pr. Bier and Pr. Schwerd, designed a helmet that took into account the types of wounds encountered.

Before the start of the battle of Verdun, 30 000 helmets were distributed in the front lines. The iconic silhouette of the German soldier was born.

This new helmet offered far greater protection against shrapnel than its French and British counterparts.

✦ A Stirnpanzer fixed to the helmet using the ventilation horns on each side. A leather strap helped keep the brow plate in place.

✦ The point in wearing a helmet in a combat zone is well illustrated here, with the helmet having visibly stopped a piece of shrapnel that would have been fatal if the soldier had been wearing a leather Pickelhaube.

✦ The liner was made up of three fabric pads filled with horse-hair. Some soldiers replaced the horse-hair with field dressings.

THE PICKELHAUBE

Its well-designed shape protected the skull efficiently and its peak left a broad field of vision. The helmet was so well designed that the Americans have used its physionomy for its current helmet, which explains why it is nicknamed «Fritz».

The helmet weighed 1 kilogram, which was perfectly bearable. The two horns on each side allowed to attach an extra armour plate, called the Stirnpanzer. This addition was quickly abandoned due to its weight. Only snipers or sentries came to use it, since they were static troops their tasks did not require any movement.

The silhouette of the helmet was instantly recognisable and it was for this reason that, as early as the winter of 1916, the Stahlhelm was camouflaged with white-coloured covers and then with hessian covers.

The painted regulation camouflage came later, in mid-1918, something which did not prevent units or individual soldiers from adding their own camouflage schemes.

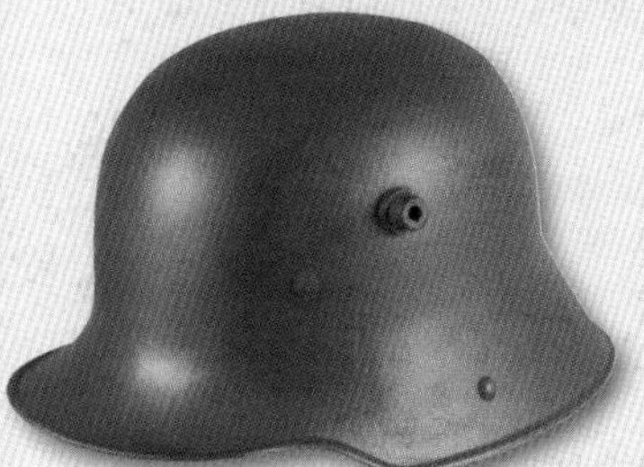

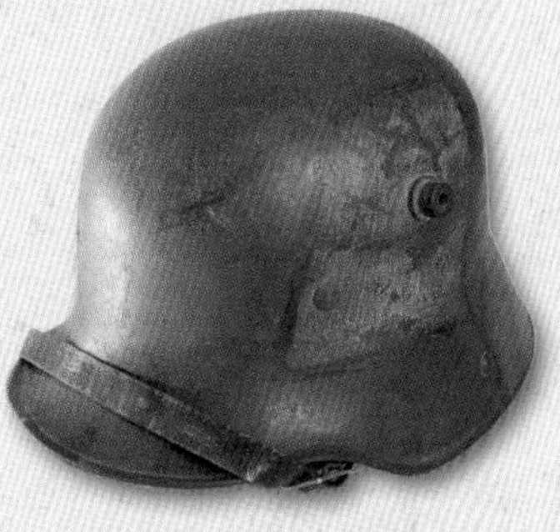

✦ Stahlhelm with its original factory-applied paint.

✦ Various camouflage schemes on 1916 helmets.

INDIVIDUAL WEAPONS : GRENADES ...

1916

✦ Egg grenade (1917), otherwise known as the Eihandgranate 17. It used a friction fuse.

✦ After its introduction in 1915, the stick grenade evolved. In 1917, ignition was carried out by unscrewing a cap at the base of the handle which freed a short string attached to a porcelain ball. One only had to pull it to make the grenade explode five seconds later. Pictured here is a Stiehlhandranate 17.

✦ 1. Kugelhandgranate 13 with a 1915 friction fuse.

✦ 2. Kugelhandgranate 15 with a 1915 friction fuse. The main difference is the fragmentation belt in the middle of the grenade, which allowed a greater splinter dispersion.

Very quickly, the infantry found themselves face to face with the enemy. Rifles proved to be far too cumbersome in the trenches, and only officers had pistols at first.

Grenades caused efficient damage while remaining undercover. They proved to have a devastating effect, especially in dug-outs where the fragmentation and blast guaranteed killing the enemy. Right from the beginning of the war, Germany was ahead of France, thanks to its fragmentation grenades that scattered splinters around them. The most famous type of grenade was the stick grenade, the Stiehlhandgranate, which was introduced in 1915. This offensive grenade had a long wooden handle and proved to be devastatingly efficient. It was easy to carry, and its handle gave leverage to throw the grenade far enough to avoid the blast and splinters.

✦ Private Josef Wilhelmy proudly wearing his combat equipment. Carrying stick grenades (pictured here are the 17 pattern) was made easier by the hook placed at the back. In 1917, Wilhemy was 31. He was mobilised in 1914 and is still wearing his Feldrock 07/10 here which appears to be in good condition. His brand-new boots probably mean that he had just been transferred to a combat unit, as the Germans had been trying to make good their losses of the past three years. It is worth noting the breadbag strap which is used to hold the ammunition pouches, whereas the haversack is missing. Josef Wilhelmy died of wounds in a hospital in Metz on 23 May 1917. He is buried in the small cemetery of his hometown Hambuch, north of Trier.

...AND COMBAT KNIVES

Meanwhile, in certain cases, close-quarter fighting was inevitable. Many soldiers took their own personal hunting knives, but other regulation models were issued too.

To advance in combat, grenades were used to clear the way and to knock out or kill enemy soldiers hidden in dug-outs.

Pistols, due to their size, were more widely used than rifles. The same went for knives and they were preferred over bayonets for the same reason - they were shorter and lighter (and thus easier to handle). Bayonets, if not fixed to the rifle, were often at risk of staying stuck in the enemy's flesh, whereas knives proved to be a lot more suited to trench combat. Knives were widely issued as early as 1915, even though many soldiers had already taken the precaution of bringing their own personal weapons, such as hunting knives. The same applied for shortened bayonets.

Sometimes, long-forgotten weapons made a come-back in the hands of the Landser, such as maces and brass knuckles that were either crafted in the trenches or purchased behind the lines.

✦ Civilian knife.
✦ Ersatz knife made entirely of steel.
✦ Regulation knife with wooden grip.
✦ Ersatz Demag bayonet-knife.
✦ Another type of regulation knife.

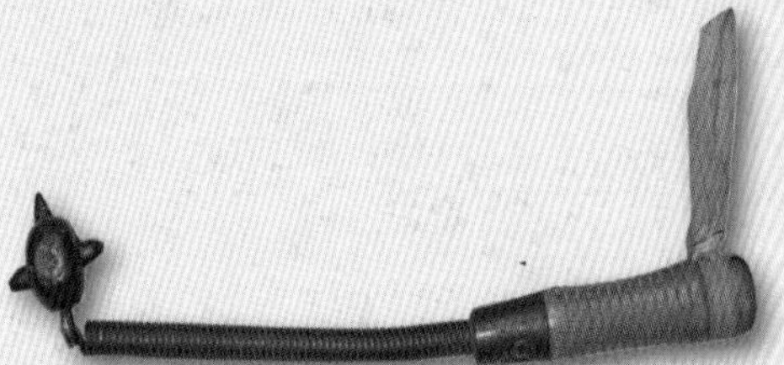

✦ A mace used by a friend's Alsatian grandfather who was mobilised into the German army.

✦ Hunting knife.

✦ For the anecdote, this Great War knife was found on a wounded German soldier in Avranches in 1944. Had this weapon been given to him by his father ?

✦ The stormtrooper's favourite weapons, consisting of the knife and 08 pistol.

1914 1915 1916 1917 1918

MG 08/15 CREW MAN : MORT-HOMME HILL, VERDUN

✦ MG 08/15 crew member wearing a Bluse 15. His regimental number present on his shoulder straps are concealed under a canvas flap for camouflage purposes. The steel helmet that had been supplied since the beginning of the year had been generalised by the time fighting reached Mort-Homme hill. The gas mask (here, a Gummimaske 15) made of rubberised canvas is placed on the chest for quick access. Indeed, the threat was real, since the Allies also used the weapon. He carries the cleaning and maintenance kit for the MG 08/15, which was bigger than the MG 08's kit, since it included all the necessary tools and spare parts. As an ammunition belt man, his rifle is a G 98, which explains the presence of a 98/05 bayonet worn on the side. This helmet clearly provided better protection, covering the base of the head as well as a broader field of vision.

✦ First 1917 pattern of the multi-section trench armour (Sappenpanzer). This pattern did not have the plate for the rifle butt on its front. Due to its 9 kilogram weight, it was not worn in combat, but was nevertheless used for static positions such as sentry duty. It is worth noting that the armour could be used with the Stirnpanzer (see page 16).

✦ DREYSE machine-guns entered the war at the same time as the MG 08/15 in late 1916, but in smaller numbers. They were a lighter and thus more mobile alternative to the MG 08.

STILL ALL QUIET ON THE WESTERN FRONT

For the Germans, 1917 started with a strategic withdrawal to the Siegfried line (otherwise known as the Hindenburg Line for the Allies), which was, due to a lack of troops, a fortified line. The battles of Verdun and the Somme, due to the huge losses they caused, had indeed greatly challenged the German army which was fighting on two main fronts.
New recruits were younger and barely made up for the losses.

It was in this context that a new French attack was launched, this time on the Chemin des Dames, on April 16th. Once again, the offensive led to a bloodbath : the preliminary artillery had failed to inflict significant damage on the Germans, who remained sheltered in their concrete dugouts, and the French were mown down by the German fire. This date also saw the French use tanks for the first time.

The Chemin des Dames proved to be too much for the French and mutinies took place in some areas, with soldiers refusing to go over the top. They could not take any more.
On the German side, the situation seemed to be improving. After its defeats in 1916, the Russian front was wavering, which led to great social trouble in the country. The Czar abdicated on March 15.

One last Russian offensive, despite a few initial successes, turned to disaster.
The autumn saw the October Revolution which placed Lenin in power : Soviet Russia was born and signed a peace treaty with Germany on December 7th.

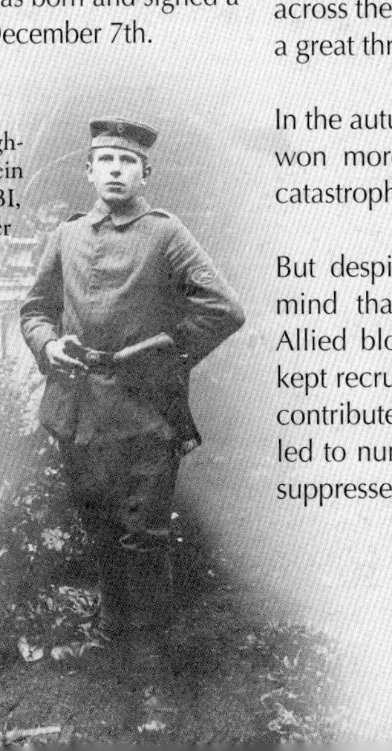

✦ The same man, after one year of fighting, has become a true Frontschwein (the German equivalent of the PBI, literally a front line pig). His mother was obviously no longer needed for this picture that was taken in the family's garden. His face seems hardened. He is proudly displaying his MG marksman insignia and the holster for his P08. His Feldrock 07/10 has been replaced by a Bluse 15 and he now wears ankle boots instead of the jackboots. The cigar in his hand gives a final war-like touch to the soldier.

✦ 1916 : huge human losses forced Germany to mobilise even younger men that had not spontaneously and patriotically joined the army before they were due to be called up. Pictured here is a freshly enlisted young man posing with his mother. She seems proud but worried, even though she is not aware of the conditions on the front line. Propaganda worked well : it glorified the soldiers and made light of the losses.

The Eastern Front was now finished and this enabled Germany to concentrate all their troops in the West.

This was just in time as the United States, in reaction to their boats being torpedoed, such as the Lusitania, had entered the conflict on April 6th, 1917. First of all, the United States were not a threat to Germany : their army was ill-equipped and had no experience in trench warfare. Moreover, transferring troops across the Atlantic was a long process. U-Boat's were a great threat and slowed down the convoys.

In the autumn, Germany and Austria-Hungary finally won more battles against Italy. The situation was catastrophic and total disaster was narrowly avoided.

But despite these victories, it is worth keeping in mind that Germany was still suffering from the Allied blockade. Food was rationed and the army kept recruiting younger and younger men. All of this contributed to undermining Germany's morale which led to numerous social upheavals that were quickly suppressed by the army.

COLLECTIVE WEAPONS

✦ A machine-gun unit posing for a picture. The ammunition suppliers' straps were used to transport the guns. The shields placed in front of the guns are clearly visible, but they were hardly ever used in combat since the guns were often used in concrete or reinforced dug-outs. This postcard, which was posted in April 1918, proves that the Feldrock 07/10 was still in use at the time along with the 15 pattern Bluse. Only the NCOs wear the ribbon of the Iron Cross 2nd Class.

Germany adopted the Maxim 1908 (Maschinen Gewehr 08) in 1908. It was an automatic weapon that used recoil to reload. Of 7.92 calibre it was fed by canvas 250-bullet ammunition belts. Its cooling system was a steel sleeve containing four litres of water, giving the gun a 500 round per minute rate of fire.

At the beginning of the war, there was one machine-gun company per regiment. Machine-guns were used in a rational way and their terrific efficiency was the cause of a great number of deaths in the summer of 1914.

The weapon gained popularity and there were three machine-gun companies per regiment by 1916. In order to adapt to the trenches, many makeshift gun mounts were made by the soldiers themselves. Weapons captured from the enemy were also re-used.

1915 saw the creation of elite machine-gun units (MG Scharfsschutzen Truppen). The members of such units were made recognisable by their sleeve insignia symbolising an MG on a mount (see photo below). Proud of belonging to such units, they often painted this insignia on their helmets.

The increasing issue of machine-guns throughout the war proves their strategic importance, in 1914 there were 5,000 machine-guns and 32,000 at the end of the war.

ACCESSORIES MG

✦ The MG 08 seen here with its mount still bearing the original paint. The pipe is part of the gun's cooling system. Ammunition cases containing 500 rounds (Patronenkasten für MG) are placed on the ground.

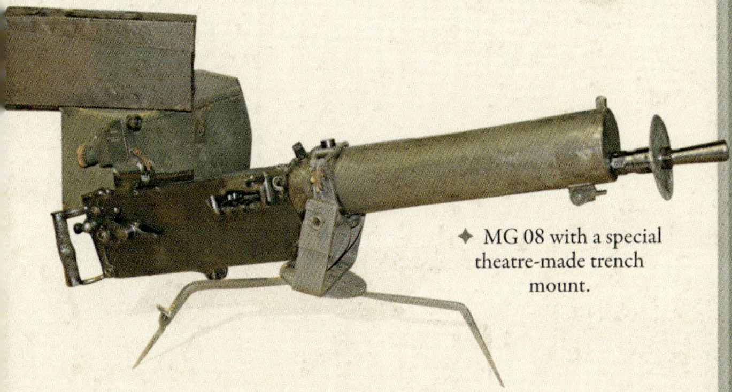

✦ MG 08 with a special theatre-made trench mount.

✦ Another example of a theatre-made gun mount. This one allowed the gun to be mounted on the trench parapet.

✦ Gun sight positioned on the left-hand side of the gun (Zielfernrohr 12) made by Emil Busch.

✦ This tool was used to fill the canvas ammunition belts with bullets.

1917

COLLECTIVE WEAPONS : THE MG 08/15

In 1915, due to the static nature of the war, the army adopted a new, lighter machine-gun : the MG 08/15. Indeed, with its sledge mount, the MG 08 weighed almost 55 kilograms and proved to be far too cumbersome to be used in offensive combat.

The MG 08/15 was mounted on a bi-pod and only weighed 18 kilograms, making it possible to be carried into captured enemy trenches and providing significant cover for the rest of the troops. It was supplied with a 100-round magazine. Approximately 127,000 were made and the weapon was a common sight on all fronts.

✦ A pouch for maintenance equipment, made here in ersatz fabric - it was previously made of leather. This pouch was worn on the belt.

✦ The same pouch, but open, revealing its contents : various tools and a spare breech.

✦ A wooden case containing accessories and various spare parts.

✦ Two drum magazines containing 100 rounds each, seen here placed on a transportation case.

✦ MG 08/15 with its drum magazine. The box at the front is a heater containing embers to prevent the water of the cooling system from freezing during the winter months. Eventually the army used glycerin instead of water during the cold season.

✦ Soldiers training with the MG 08/15. The ammunition belt feeder's role is clearly illustrated here. By holding the belt, the gun is less prone to jamming.

NCO MACHINE-GUN CREW COMMANDER

✦ 1910 pattern officer's cap.

✦ A Lederschutzmaske 17 gas mask, presented here with its sheet metal transportation case, its instruction manual and the canvas pouch containing a spare filter that was carried on the belt. From now on, it was not to be carried in the canvas pouch.

✦ A case for MG ammunition (Patronenkaste 10), containing two belts of 250 rounds each. The markings on the case indicate the regiment (Res JR 103, that is to say the 103rd reserve infantry regiment from Saxony. These cases were transported in carts in order to supply the MGs with bullets. MW signifies Munitionwagen.

✦ Rangefinders (Entfernungsmesser 14) were used to determine the distance of the target and to thus adjust fire.

✦ The members of the elite MG units were so proud of their units that their helmets were also painted with the MG insignia.

✦ This non-commissioned officer (rank insignia on collar) was part of an MG unit of the 64th inf.regt. that was attached to the 6th infantry division which fought on the Chemin des Dames in 1917. Since the NCOs were the gun commanders, they ordered when to open fire, adjusted fire and chose targets. This explains why they were equipped with binoculars (Fernglas), pictured here in a leather Case fixed at the belt, as well as a P08 and a knife with a wrist-strap for close-quarter combat. The breadbag strap holds everything in place when the haversack is not worn. Personal torches tended to be worn on the tunic. The cap in the picture has had its red band covered with canvas for camouflage reasons.

THE GERMANS AT THE GATES OF PARIS ONCE MORE

1918 started well for Germany. The front line was still in a stalemate as the last allied offensives had failed to break through, but both sides were nevertheless exhausted by this war of attrition that had already caused the deaths of more than 1.1 million soldiers by that point.

The peace treaty with Russia signed in Brest-Litovsk on 18 March enabled Germany to concentrate all their troops on the Western Front, bringing the number of German divisions present up to 172, against the 174 allied divisions.

The 21 March saw a return to war of movement with the launching of the Ludendorff offensive. The British were forced to retreat, opening a gap in allied lines, but General Foch, now the supreme allied commander, succeeded in avoiding total disaster by stopping the offensive on April 5th.

A new German offensive took place on 27 May on the Chemin des Dames. The Germans crossed the Marne river at Château-Thierry on 30 May. But once again, thanks to US divisions, the offensive was contained quickly, on 5 June, only 65 kilometers away from Paris.

Germany attacked once more on July 15th with the Friedensturm offensive that was thwarted by the Allies who had heard rumours of a planned offensive through the interrogation of many prisoners of war. A counter-attack was launched as early as 18 July, wiping out the German advance : the second Battle of the Marne was won.

Then, on 8 August, an allied offensive was launched in Picardy. This day became «the black day of the German army".

Tanks and aviation were being used more and more by the Allies during offensive phases. Germany drew many important conclusions from this experience, conclusions that would bear fruit 21 years later ...

From this moment on, the Axis powers knew that the war was lost. Austria-Hungary and the Ottoman Empire were crumbling under Allied attacks.

Fighting was still raging on in France however, particularly in the Aisne and Ardennes regions.

Germany was in a painful situation, its civilians and soldiers were suffering increasingly from the blockade that had caused terrible food shortages for both soldiers and civilians. The Russian revolution inspired social and revolutionary movements in Germany, undermining central power. Despite being underfed, exhausted and vulnerable to disease such as the fast-spreading Spanish flu epidemic, the soldiers resisted bravely. However, on 7 November the first peace talks took place and led to the signing of the armistice in Rethondes on 11 November.

In addition to the dreadful human losses (1.95 million deaths), the treaty of Versailles imposed draconian conditions on Germany, especially in geographic terms, with the loss of the Alsace-Lorraine and of their colonial Empire, as well as economically with utterly unachievable war reparations.

Contrary to France, Germany did not suffer from material destruction, but the Diktat of Versailles exacerbated German nationalism, creating the conditions that favoured the election in 1933 of an ex-corporal of the imperial army called Adolf Hitler.

✦ These soldiers have written «I did not want the war» on an unexploded shell. Their serious faces are a testimony of their exhaustion after four years of fighting.

THE STURMTRUPPEN

With the war of position that started in 1915, the German army had to adapt to new ways of fighting. New units, composed of daring soldiers, were created for nocturnal, rapid and pin-point attacks to capture sentries or to destroy enemy outposts and strategically placed machine-gun nests. This new type of soldier learnt a new way of fighting with light equipment and weaponry, such as grenades and handguns.

These units were the ancestors of the Sturm battalions that were created in 1916 by Captain Rohr, an officer who broke new ground in terms of fighting tactics. These new tactics were successful, leading to the capture of the Hartmannswillerkopf in late 1915, for instance, during which the first Sturm-Abteilung showed what they were capable of.

In 1918, the German army fielded 56 Sturm-Divisions during the Ludendorff offensive that broke through and infiltrated the Franco-British defences.

However, the troops were exhausted and worn down by severe losses and the offensive ended on 4 June.

Afterwards, the Sturmtruppen were sent to various sectors on the front line when needed in an emergency and were unable to prevent Germany's defeat.
These soldiers were generally very fit and well-equipped, their extensive training also familiarised them with all kinds of weapons from grenades to flame-throwers.

The basic rifle used by the Sturmtruppen was the Kar.98 A, which was shorter and easier to handle than the Gew98. The P08 was also supplied as well as stick grenades contained in large bags made by the units themselves. Defensive grenades, being small, were carried in the pockets of the Bluse. It was also essential to have wire cutters to break through barbed wire, and a large shovel used to dig in on captured enemy positions.

Their trousers were modified with leather padding on the knees. Their boots and puttees were also more better suited to their role than the jackboot. The Sturmtruppen worked hand in hand with the artillery which facilitated their progress by eliminating pockets of resistance.

✦ Sturmtruppen in training. The soldiers pictured here are experienced since many of them have the Iron Cross ribbon. Their faces show determination, and the perspective of a German defeat does not seem to have affected them. Once again, we can see that peacetime and wartime issued tunics were both used at this point in the war.

THE INFANTRYMAN OF THE LUDENDORFF OFFENSIVE

✦ A typical MG ammunition carrier, with transportation straps worn over the shoulder and an MG maintenance kit (see contents page 24). The Bluse 15 and the camouflaged helmet give an idea of what a German soldier would have looked like in 1918.

1915 1916 1917

1918

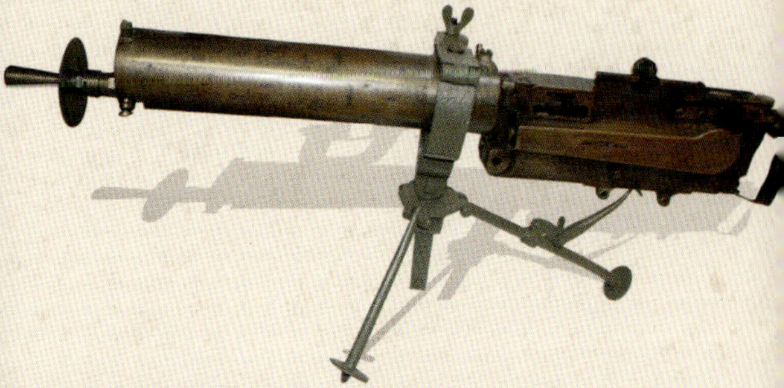

✦ MG 08 on a theatre-made trench mount.

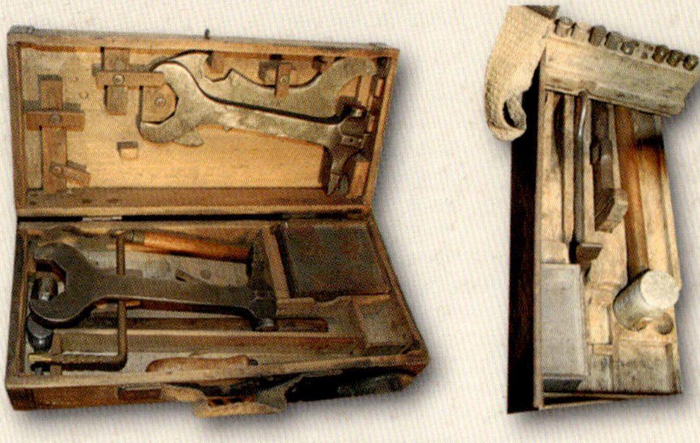

✦ Two different models of tool kits both used by MG armourers to dismantle and repair the guns in a combat zone.

✦ The A7V tank (Sturmpanzerwagen) failed to bring victory to Germany. The one pictured here has been toppled over (the turret is visible) and captured by the French. It is probably the 527 'LOTTI' tank used by lieutenant Bergemann during the attack near Reims on June 1st that got stuck in a trench before flipping on to its side. It was subsequently hit by artillery. Abandoned by its crew, it was broken up for scrap metal in 1922.

A NEW WEAPON: TANKS

Tanks were first used by the British in September 1916 during the Battle of the Somme. These new vehicles failed to contribute significantly to the fighting since they were prone to mechanical problems.

On the other hand, Germans met the tanks with stupor and terror as these large steel monsters armed with machine-guns and guns seemed unstoppable. Tanks had a devastating effect on enemy morale thanks to their apparent invincibility.

However, the Germans reacted quickly and used their artillery to stop the tanks.

As a consequence, the first use of tanks by the French at Berry au Bac during the Chemin des Dames in 1917 was a failure. They suffered from mechanical breakdowns and the battle ended with a battlefield strewn with carcasses of tanks that had been destroyed by artillery fire.

1918 saw tanks being used in large-scale offensives. The Renault FT 17 tanks were used in great numbers, especially during the battle of Saint Mihiel in September. The Americans used 267 of them as well as the Saint Chamond and Schneider tanks that were obsolete at that time.

Germany, however, was behind the Allies in terms of armoured vehicles. Around twenty A7V tanks were produced and used alongside captured enemy tanks. The lessons drawn from this experience were taken into account during the Blitzkrieg at the beginning of the Second World War.

The only anti-tank weapon supplied to the infantry was the 13mm calibre Tankgewehr, a crossover between a small artillery piece and a rifle. 13,500 of them were made and supplied from May 1918 onwards.

✦ These three pictures represent British Mark IV tanks, the most commonly used by the British Army. Many of them that had been destroyed or damaged by artillery fire during the battle of Cambrai were repaired and re-used by the Germans.

TRENCH ARTILLERY

Trench warfare limited the use of traditional artillery guns as their flat trajectory made them unusable without appropriate protection.

The Germans used three types of mortars (Minenwerfer) as early as 1914, with 25, 21 and 17mm calibres developed following the Russo-Japanese war (1904-1905) ; mortars had indeed been instrumental in the siege and capture of Port Arthur.

The mortars' curved trajectory of fire were particularly well suited to the trenches. When brought close to the enemy they could cause significant damage due to the heavy explosive charge contained in the shell (a 120 kilogram projectile, of which 30 kg was explosive with a range of 300 metres).

The British and the French were at a loss when faced with this type of weapon that they did not possess. Their first reaction was to put back into service 50-year old siege mortars or to manufacture makeshift weapons such as catapults for launching grenades.

The German army, however, had military pioneer units specialised in the use of Minenwerfers. Their numbers increased throughout the war.

Other than these large-calibre mortars, many grenade launchers (Granatwerfer) also existed. They were a lot easier to handle and lighter to carry.

✦ In order to underline his belonging to a Minenwerfer unit, this soldier has drawn a firing mortar on the rear underside of his helmet.

✦ On the Champagne front, in April 1917.

MEDALS AND AWARDS

Just like all the other belligerents, Germany offered various awards to its most deserving soldiers, the most famous being the Iron Cross (Eisernes Kreuz).

Created by Frederick Wilhelm III of Prussia in 1813 during the Napoleonic wars, the Iron Cross was reinstated by Wilhelm II on 5 August 1914.

There were two distinct categories : Second-Class crosses were not worn in combat : only the black and white ribbon was present, on the tunic, close to the buttonhole. It was awarded without distinction of rank or social class, and was thus very popular among soldiers, just like the Croix de Guerre in France. Approximately 5 million of them were awarded during the war.

First Class Iron Crosses were wearable in combat as they had a pin that allowed it to be worn on the chest, on the left-hand side. Only 218,000 of them were awarded, mostly to officers.
The Pour le Mérite, far more prestigious and almost exclusive to superior officers, was created in 1740 by Frederick II of Prussia. It remained the highest German award throughout the war.

Finally, the Wound Badge was created on 3 March 1918, and awarded to soldiers who had been wounded in combat. It was black if the soldier in question had one wound, and silver for three or four wounds.

After the war, many commemorative medals were created to honour the soldiers. The most commonly awarded one was the Ehrenkreuz, also known as the Hindenburg Cross.

✦ A soldier of the 119th inf.regt. displaying his 2nd class ribbon.

✦ A 1st Class Iron Cross with a round plate to attach it to the tunic.

✦ A 1st class Iron Cross.

✦ A typical post-war set of decorations comprising of a 2nd Class Iron Cross with its ribbon and a commemorative 1914-1918 Ehrenkreutz worn by Great War veterans. These medals belonged to Gefreiter Ternes whose Militarpass is seen on page 5.

✦ A black Wound Badge (Verwundetenabzeichnen).

✦ The Iron Cross, the ultimate patriotic symbol, was present on many objects such as this metal box, but also on aircraft and tanks as nationality markers.

1918 1917

CONCLUSION

Other than extreme material damage, the war caused the deaths of about 1.95 million German soldiers.

Even though many were able to be buried, many bodies have never been found, pulverised by the intense violence of the conflict.

To this day, German military cemeteries across the globe are managed and maintained by the Deutsche Kriegsgräberfürsorge.
A website is available to help find a soldier's grave : http://volksbund.de, on the "Gräbersuche" page. By entering a family name, the website will give you the exact location of the grave.

Sadly, many archives were destroyed during the Second World War and many soldiers have never been given a grave : some are still in the ground, some have been found but without their identity tags and re-buried in ossuaries.

Anton Schmitt, for example, was born in 1891 in the village of Hambuch, north of Trier. Taken prisoner in September 1914, he spent two years as a P.O.W. in Morocco before returning to France, where he succumbed to the influenza epidemic on 18 November 1918.

His temporary grave is pictured on the following page. The Volksbund website indicates that Anton Schmitt lays at rest in Cernay cemetery in the Alsace, block 1, grave number 267.

For further research, it is possible to use the Wast, in Berlin : Deutsche Dienstelle WAST Eichborndamm 179 D-13403 Berlin.

Despite the destruction caused by WWII, many military archives have survived. However, access to these files are only authorised to family members.
Moreover, if you ever come across identity tags, please contact the Volksbund - the owner's body may not be far away, and finding it will be a comfort to relatives.

✦ Anton Schmitt photographed in Koblenz before leaving for the war.

✦ Anton Schmitt in captivity - see the PG markings (PG = Prisonnier de Guerre) on his tunic and trousers. He was able to send this card along with a message to his family.